IMAGES
of Sport

BLACKHEATH FC
RUGBY FOOTBALL CLUB

Compiled by
Dave Hammond

TEMPUS

First published 1999
Copyright © Dave Hammond, 1999

Tempus Publishing Limited
The Mill, Brimscombe Port,
Stroud, Gloucestershire, GL5 2QG

ISBN 0 7524 1688 X

Typesetting and origination by
Tempus Publishing Limited
Printed in Great Britain by
Midway Clark Printing, Wiltshire

Present and Forthcoming Rugby Union *Images* titles from Tempus Publishing:

Cardiff Rugby Football Club 1876-1939
Cardiff Rugby Football Club 1939-2000
Newport Rugby Football Club 1874-1950
Newport Rugby Football Club 1950-2000
Llanelli Rugby Football Club

Also available from Tempus:

The Complete Five Nations Story by David Hands (hardback £19.99)

IMAGES
of Sport

BLACKHEATH FC
RUGBY FOOTBALL CLUB

Blackheath's Rectory Field nestles in the heart of South East London, just to the south of the Thames and the Millennium Dome. Options to extend the facilities are limited because it is a designated green field site. The setting is, nevertheless, very picturesque and tranquil – a perfect place for Saturday afternoon family entertainment.

Contents

Introduction   7

1.   First Seeds and Early Growth   9

2.   The Rectory Field   21

3.   Representative Games   33

4.   Barbarians and the Touring Tradition   49

5.   The World's Premier Club   65

6.   Struggling with the New Order   83

7.   The Short Game – Rugby Sevens   107

8.   The Old and the Beautiful   115

9.   The Future's Bright in Red and Black   123

Acknowledgements   128

The author Dave Hammond (on the right) with club president Sir Hal Miller, peruse Dave's earlier prose-based book on Blackheath. This book and *The Club* were designed to compliment each other.

Introduction

Blackheath Rugby Club, or more properly Blackheath Football Club, hold a very special place in the history of the game of rugby. Not only is it the oldest open club in existence, it and its representatives have played a significant part in the development of the game, locally, nationally and on an international basis.

The club may not be at the pinnacle of the game at the moment, but any other club still has a long way to go before it can claim an international playing list as long as that of 'The Club'. Over 240 players have represented their country while on the books of this world famous side. Men connected with Blackheath founded the Football Association, the Rugby Football Union, the Army Rugby Union and the Barbarians, just to name a few achievements. Internationals and Varsity matches were played on their home pitch and individual players have been responsible for re-shaping the game – the first specialist hooker was a Blackheath man, as was the first recognised wing-forward.

It is amazing that while the club is renowned throughout the world of rugby its history has never been told in one volume. A number of pamphlets have been produced over the years dealing briefly with certain stages of the club's past, but it has never been pulled together. As far as the local community has been concerned the club has dipped in popularity to such a degree that many in the area are even unsure as to where they play. Some, without having visited the Rectory Field, feel that rugby is a game played by and for an elite few.

This is all very shameful. The history of rugby union cannot be told without multiple references to Blackheath, and I believe that it is impossible to recount the history of Blackheath without a good look at the men who have worn the red and black hoops – world famous sportsmen like C.B. Fry and Andrew Stoddart as well as more recent local personalities, such as Mickey Skinner.

Established by former pupils of Blackheath Proprietary School, the club started playing on the heath just north of the village. From there they moved a half-mile away to a place on Old Dover Road (now occupied by shops) and eventually they moved to The Rectory Field on the border of Blackheath and Charlton. Those early pioneers of the game established themselves as the best, both at playing and organising the game of rugby; they forged the first ever Anglo-Welsh links and they facilitated the first ever Scotland *v.* England game. Rugby would have developed without the input of Blackheath, but it is hard to imagine exactly how.

I first decided that the history of Blackheath FC was a worthwhile project very soon after making my initial visit to the Rectory Field in 1994. As a life-long supporter of Charlton Athletic I was one of those unsure as to where the Rectory Field was. I was also unsure of the sort of reception that I would get on visiting the clubhouse. The club had a reputation of being very insular, and my accent is decidedly South East London, rather than public school! However, my concerns were ill founded: Blackheath Rugby Club is a wonderful place filled with marvellous characters. I was and am very welcome, as are you. I have made many friends, visited many grounds and travelled the length and breadth of the country with the team.

Despair there has been aplenty, perhaps made all the worse by knowledge of the greatness of the club's past, but I have followed a promotion-winning team and I am convinced that the club will rise again to great heights. More to the point, I have enjoyed the experience immensely. Once I decided that I would write the club's history I was discouraged by many people. The club's records had been destroyed by fire during the Second World War, there was a hotly contested dispute about the actual date of the club's inception and there was definitely no budget. Not afraid of hard work, and being a journalist, I was not to be put off. I quickly acquired the support of the club's archivist Hugh Brodie and the help of a senior member, Peter Brown.

'Brownie' was far more interested in the photographs than I was at that stage. While I felt that there was a great story to be told, he felt that it could be told in pictures. He came along with me to see countless former members of the club and wrote a string of letters to relatives of deceased players, seeking out information. At various places, while I was going through old documents he would be quietly going through the photographs, hoping that he would be able to persuade me into having a bigger photographic section than I had originally intended. We spoke about doing a pictorial history to run alongside or after the text-based work we were putting together, but I was fearful of costs and lacked any technical knowledge. Then came a conversation with Tempus Publishing and here you have it – the history of Blackheath FC in pictures.

Memories are there to be shared and without pictures it becomes a little harder to do that. Blackheath have a collective memory that is quite simply glorious. It is one that should enthral anybody connected with rugby and hopefully it will inspire greater things to come – 'Come on The Club'!

One
First Seeds and Early Growth

Little is known about the precise origins of the game of rugby football, but before the inception of Blackheath FC there were a number of 'closed' clubs in existence, operating for the benefit of members of certain schools, old boys or professions. Blackheath's origins are in the Proprietary School that had previously existed in the village. The school's badge was used by Blackheath members right up until the 1950s, despite the fact that the school closed down in 1907.

The Blackheath Proprietary School was established in 1831 for the benefit of local boys, most of the other schools in the area being boarding establishments. The school was funded by the selling of 100 shares at £20 each. The site of the original building is now occupied by Selwyn Court, with St Joseph's Academy a few hundred yards away.

Many of the boys from the Proprietary School were keen on sports, but the rules did not allow the playing of them on school premises. The boys therefore went over onto the heath to play their favoured games – hockey and football.

BLACKHEATH

PROPRIETARY SCHOOL.

INSTITUTED 1830.

MDCCCLXXX.

LONDON:
PRINTED BY R. CLAY, SONS, AND TAYLOR,
BREAD STREET HILL, QUEEN VICTORIA STREET.

The team very quickly gained itself a reputation of rough and uncompromising play. Hacking (the kicking of an opponent's shins) was allowed up until 1871 and Blackheath were one of the greatest exponents of such play. This picture is of the school side of 1866/67 and it is highly probable that some of these players went on to play for Blackheath FC.

R. E. GOWER.

...THE FOUNDERS...

of the

Blackheath

Football

Club.

ALEX. SINCLAIR.

JOHN C. SINCLAIR.

The old boys of Blackheath had been playing together since 1858 and come 1862 they were ready to form themselves into a properly constituted 'open' club, allowing players other than former pupils to join. All the original officers of the club were, however, former boys from the school.

The first captain of Blackheath was William Burnett. In true Blackheath traditions, Burnett, who had also captained the school team, went on to be a major influence on the development of the game. An Australian by birth he moved to New Zealand where he continued to be influential in the world of rugby.

The first ever team picture of the side shows all the original committeemen except Burnett as still playing. This picture is purported to be of the 1862 side, but is possibly slightly older. The players provided the red and black hooped shirts at their own cost. No nails or gutta percha were allowed in the boots. From left to right, back row: Sir R.G. Head, W. Dawes, W. Gower, F. Campbell, W. Bischoff, C. Moore, W. Smith, L. Sueur. Front row: A. Mitchell, T. Dawes, A. Poynder.

BLACKHEATH FOOTBALL CLUB.

NULLI SECUNDUS

FOUNDED

WILLIAM BURNETT·
— BLACKHEATH —
FIRST CAPTAIN

1 8 0 0

ALEX: SINCLAIR·
BLACKHEATH

JOHN. C. SINCLAIR·
BLACKHEATH

THE FOUNDERS AND A TEAM OF THE BLACKHEATH FOOTBALL CLUB
IN 1862

1 Sir R.G. HEAD, Bart   MARLBOROUGH
2 W. DAWES   BLACKHEATH
3 W.L. GOWER   DO
4 F.M. CAMPBELL   DO
5 W. BISCHOFF   RUGBY

6 C. MOORE   NEW ZEALAND
7 W.F. SMITH   BLACKHEATH
8 L.P. SUEUR   — DO —
9 ALEX: MITCHELL   MARLBOROUGH
10 T. DAWES   BLACKHEATH
11 A. POYNDER   — DO —

R.E. GOWER·

·FOUNDERS·

13

Among those who played for Blackheath in the early days was Francis Maule Campbell. Campbell was the Blackheath representative that attended the first meetings of the fledgling Football Association in 1863 on behalf of the club. He was elected as the FA's first ever treasurer, but led the Blackheath walk out when it was agreed by the committee to ban hacking.

The Princess of Wales public house was used as a changing room for many of the teams that played on the heath, including Blackheath. One of the other sides that used the building was Guy's Hospital. Guy's lost many of their better players to Blackheath, due, presumably, to friendships that developed in the bar after games. To this day the pub still has a room adorned with memorabilia of Blackheath FC.

The pub's owners finally acknowledged their establishment's significance in the history of The Club when it unveiled two plaques in 1992. This picture shows Sir Brian Jenkins and Mick Skinner pulling the cords. To Skinner's left is Hugh Neeley, the president of The Club and a former player. To the right of Jenkins is Terry Waite and Welsh international player Cliff Morgan.

Representing Blackheath at the Pall Mall meeting, which set up the Rugby Football Union, was Frederic Stokes. Frederic was one of three rugby-playing brothers at Blackheath. He captained England in the first ever international game at Raeburn Place in Edinburgh and three times thereafter. He was captain of Blackheath from 1869 to 1872 and was elected President of the RFU in 1875, whilst still only twenty-four years of age.

Lennard Stokes, the younger brother of Frederic, became something of a legend in the world of rugby. Like his brother, Lennard captained both Blackheath and England, also rising to the post of president of the RFU. An energetic man, he was also involved in the organisation of Kent County rugby. A drop-goal specialist, Stokes was extremely popular and a man of vision both on and off the pitch.

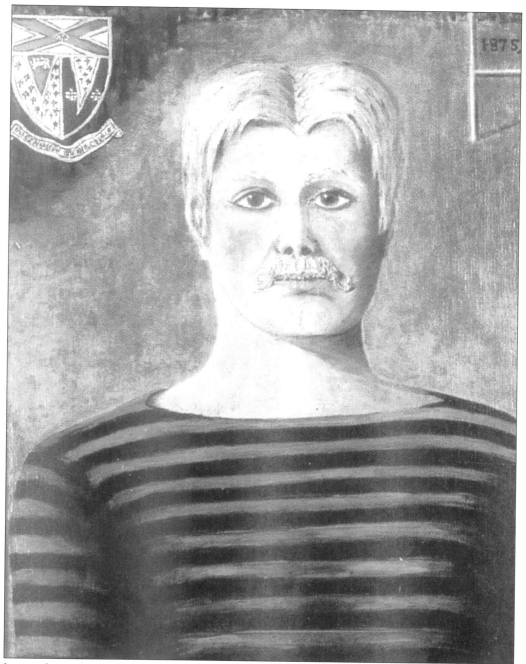

Lennard was the inspiration for Conan Doyle's Dr Watson character in the Sherlock Holmes books. Like Watson, Stokes was a surgeon from Guy's Hospital. He was captain of the club side in 1875/76. A useful all-round sportsman, being particularly good at cricket, like his brother he was also active behind the scenes of the club.

Another important character in the early history of Blackheath was Maurice Richardson. Richardson had played rugby for the Gypsies, based in Peckham, before coming over to Blackheath in 1874. When the club had to leave the heath because of crowd problems in 1877 Richardson got his father to lease the club a field just to the north. Called (appropriately enough) Richardson's Field, the site is now occupied by shops in Old Dover Road.

In 1866 the first ever county match was organised between Kent and Sussex. The Green Man, located at the top of Blackheath Hill until its demolition in 1970, became the headquarters of the county organisation.

G.W. Burton was a prime mover in the
establishment of a county rugby scene. A
strong forward player he represented
Blackheath, Kent and England. He had played
with distinction in the first ever Kent v. Surrey
fixture and went on to become secretary of
Blackheath.

Rowland Hill, who was a leading
figure in the RFU, played just once
for Blackheath, in 1885. However,
he was on the board of the parent
club. A very hard-working man he
was secretary of both the Kent RFU
and the Rugby Football Union. He
was very outspoken against the
payment of players.

For many years annual pictures were taken of the team. This picture, showing the side of 1880/81 with a number of important people from the club's history, was taken on the occasion of The Club's away fixture against Manchester. Of those included in this picture, G.W. Burton, L. Stokes, F. Stokes, A. Poland and A. Spurling were all present at the first ever meeting of the board of directors of Blackheath Cricket, Football and Lawn Tennis Club held in 1885.

Two

The Rectory Field

When Blackheath had to move out of Richardson's Field in 1883 it was Lennard Stokes that knew of a field on Charlton Road that would be a suitable ground to play on. Stokes, along with Burton, went to see Revd Swainson, the Rector of St Luke's church, Charlton and arranged for the club to play at a site leased to the church by Maryon Wilson of Charlton House.

In 1885, the Morden Cricket Club approached Blackheath to see if they could also use the Rectory Field. The Blackheath Football, Cricket and Lawn Tennis Club was established from this approach, ensuring that the Rectory Field would host more than just rugby. Since then squash has been added to the sports that are enjoyed at the site.

The representative of Morden Cricket Club, Montague Druitt, became the company's first honourable secretary. Druitt, who was a teacher in Blackheath, was one of the prime police suspects in the Jack the Ripper murder inquires of 1888. His body was found in the Thames at the time the murders stopped.

On taking over the Rectory Field, Blackheath appointed one George Street as assistant groundsman. There followed four generations of the Street family working as groundsmen at the Rectory Field. Here, Charlie's son, Bert, talks with Peter Brown in his home, which is something of a shrine to the Rectory Field, past and present.

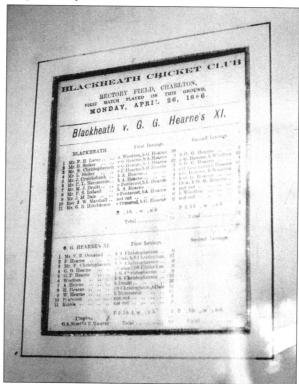

The first cricket match played on the new field took place between Blackheath and a select team. Both sides contained a Christopherson – Sidney for Blackheath, Percy for the Select XI. The Christopherson family was heavily involved in rugby and cricket. One of the ten brothers was on the original board of the limited company. At times the whole family, father and sons, would play cricket as a team.

The Cricket Club has always been an important part of the set up at the Rectory Field. There have also been many players that have played both rugby and cricket. Malcolm Christopherson (seated third from left) can be seen in this 1902 picture. The building in the background is the tennis hut, which occupied the site now taken by the north car park. The Christopherson family had been involved with Blackheath cricket and rugby since before the establishment of the Rectory Field. A descendent of the family is still a member of the club.

The pavilion was built in 1886. Even while at Richardson's Field the players had used the Princess of Wales public house as a changing room. This picture was taken in the 1970s, but the basic structure has remained the same since its opening. Note the new changing rooms added on the right hand side of the building.

Part of the groundsman's job was to wash the players' kit. This was a regular duty carried out by Charlie Street. Another of the head groundsman's tasks was to bowl for cricketers wishing to practice their batting.

The stand in this picture is very similar to, if longer than, the one currently in place at the Rectory Field. The building in the foreground is a tea hut situated on the Charlton Road side of the pavilion.

The original stand was damaged by fire during a cricket match in 1922 and was replaced that year. This picture, taken from the Cherry Orchard end, shows the fire-damaged stand. The glass-fronted construction at the end of the stand is the press box.

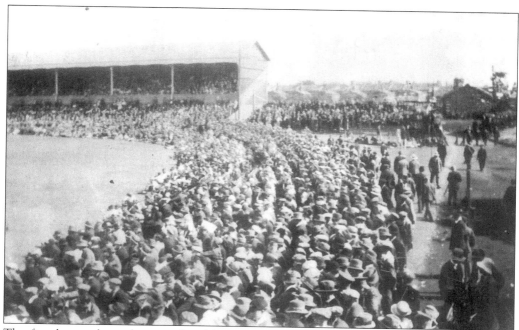

The fire-damaged stand was replaced by a two-tier construction for the start of the 1922/23 season. In those early days the Rectory Field was a popular venue and the 6,000 capacity stand was often full for cricket, as can be seen in these two pictures from the 1930s. At this time the Rectory Field was home to the Kent County Cricket Club.

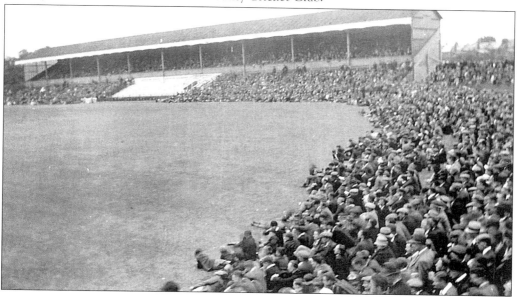

These two pictures show that the stand was not always full for rugby in the 1920s and '30s however. *Above*: Supporters huddle in the rain for a 1926 fixture against Cambridge University. *Below*: Straw is used as protection against severe frost during a fixture against Leicester in 1933.

During the Second World War the Rectory Field tea hut was used as a billet for those maintaining the barrage balloons. Charlie Street is seen here cutting the grass on the cricket square after hostilities had ceased. The pitch was not available for play until the December of 1946.

Rope seats were provided on the north side of the pitch, spectators being charged extra to sit on them. The pallets stacked behind the seats were placed on the floor for people to stand on during matches. The little boy in the foreground is, inevitably, a member of the Street family.

The Blackheath Tennis Club, as part of the set up at the Rectory Field, has always enjoyed social integration with the other clubs. In this picture of around 1948, tennis players enjoy afternoon tea while a cricket match is being played in the background.

With rugby and cricket being all-male games until recently, the members of the tennis club provided the Rectory Field with most of its female members. This picture, also of around 1948, shows that the tennis club was patronised by players of both sexes.

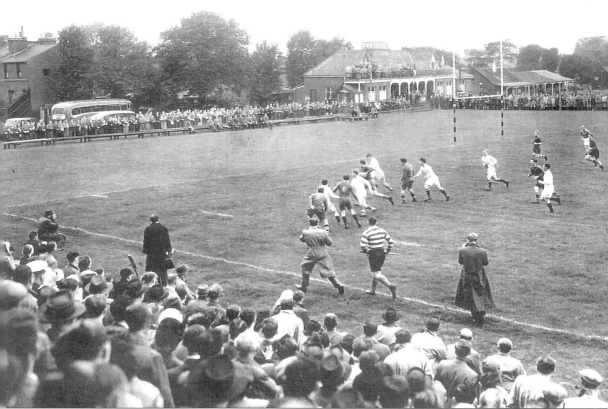

Despite a gradual decline of the public interest in rugby generally and Blackheath in particular, the Rectory Field remained a popular venue for attractive fixtures. Viewing from the pavilion roof was for members only in 1951 when this picture was taken. It is a far cry from the few hundred that attend current first team fixtures. Access to the roof is now cut off for safety reasons. The place to the left of the pavilion, where the bus is parked, is now occupied by a burger stall, offices and hospitality suites. Note that even by this time there was no padding on the posts.

Although County Cricket is no longer played at the Rectory Field, the Blackheath Cricket Club remains in situ. This recent picture was taken from inside the pavilion after an extension had been added. Note the floodlight pylon to the right of the picture.

The current stand was built to replace the two-tier stand that was bomb damaged during the Second World War. It was not erected until the 1970s. In the 1990s, the wooden plank seats were replaced with plastic bucket seats, the planks now being used for standing along the opposite touchline.

Three
Representative Games

Blackheath have had more players play for their country than any other side – over 240 to date. Men from the club have also led, as captains or managers, no less than five British Lions touring sides. This blazer badge belonged to Tony Horton, the last Club player to play for the Lions while still with Blackheath.

The Club facilitated the very first international rugby match, played at Raeburn Place in Edinburgh, home of Edinburgh Academicals, in 1871. Blackheath provided four players and the team was led by Fred Stokes. The game was the catalyst for the establishment of the Rugby Football Union and the man who responded to the Scottish challenge to organise the game was the Blackheath Secretary B.H. Burns, seated in the front row. Burns was a Scot who had previous connections with the Accies. Note that the picture shows twenty players, all of which took to the field at the kick-off. It wasn't until later that the RFU settled on the fifteen-a-side format. Playing twenty-a-side was called 'big-side' games.

In 1879 Blackheath accepted a challenge from Newport to be the first ever English side to play in Wales. They won the game easily, despite the fact that Newport as an undefeated Welsh side had the nickname of 'The Invincibles'. Two years later, in February 1881, Blackheath's Richardson's Field home was the venue for the first ever England *v.* Wales match. England won by eight goals and five tries to nil, with Lennard Stokes as captain. Harry Vassall, another Blackheath man, scored three tries. Since then, England/Wales fixtures have remained an important part of the rugby calendar, while most rugby clubs still relish the Anglo-Welsh games as events that contain hard rugby followed by friendships formed in hard drinking!

The issuing of international caps is a tradition as long as the game is old. Originally the caps were worn during games and they have always been prized possessions. The Welsh cap (above) was issued to commemorate the first ever England v. Wales international at the Rectory Field. The English cap (below) was issued to another Blackheath player, Bonaventura, in 1931.

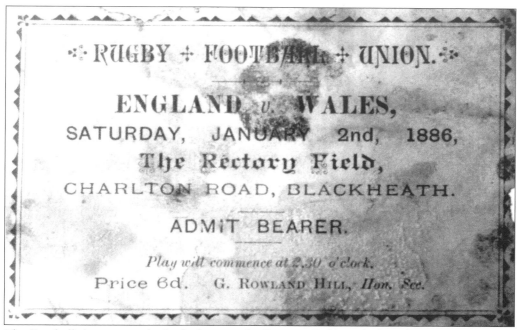

RUGBY ✠ FOOTBALL ✠ UNION.

ENGLAND *v.* WALES,

SATURDAY, JANUARY 2nd, 1886,

The Rectory Field,

CHARLTON ROAD, BLACKHEATH.

ADMIT BEARER.

Play will commence at 2.30 o'clock.

Price 6d. G. Rowland Hill, *Hon. Sec.*

The Football Association had asked to use the Rectory Field pitch for a fixture on 1 January 1886, but had been turned down because of the rugby fixture against Wales the next day. At the time Rowland Hill was RFU secretary, while the president was Lennard Stokes.

Even after leaving Richardson's Field, which was recognised as a magnificent pitch, Blackheath continued to host international fixtures. At the time of this picture Blackheath's average attendance of 2,000 was roughly the same as that of Arsenal, who played in the same area. However, the turn-out for this international game would have been over 10,000.

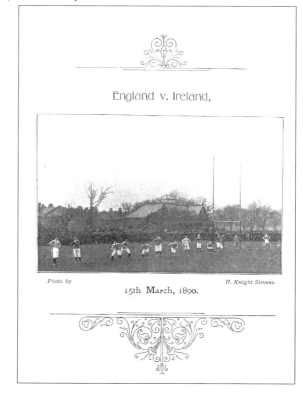

England v. Ireland,

Photo by   *H. Knight Stevens.*

15th March, 1890.

This England side that faced Wales in 1892 were easy masters of their opponents, winning 17-0. Hubbard (fifth from left, back row), Evershed (sixth from left, back row) and Allport (extreme right, middle row) were all Blackheath men.

Action photographs were not so practical in those days, newspapers often relying on artistic impressions for visual effect. This illustration shows another England try against Wales at a packed Rectory Field during the same match.

This Irish side of 1894, pictured in front of the Rectory Field pavilion, claimed an unbeaten record. Note that as late as the time this photograph was taken, the shape of the ball was still more spherical than egg shaped. Balls continued to vary in shape, according to what was available, for some time.

The England team that faced Ireland that day contained Allport, Tucker, De Winton and Byrne of Blackheath. It was captained by the great Dickie Lockwood, who later committed the heinous crime of joining the newly formed Northern Rugby League.

Rugby Football Union.

RECTORY FIELD, BLACKHEATH.

ENGLAND v. IRELAND.

Saturday, February 3, 1894.   Kick-off 3 p.m.

England.

Back:
J .F. Byrne

Three-quarter-backs:
S. Murfitt   C. A. Hooper   R. E. Lockwood (Capt.)   F. Firth

Half-backs:
R. F. C. de Winton   E. W. Taylor

J. Toothill   T. Broadley   H. Bradshaw   H. Speed

J. Hall   W. E. Tucker   A. Allport   F. Soane

RIGHT.   LEFT.

Ireland.

H. Lindsay   C. V. Rooke   J. H. Lytle   J. Lytle

G. Walmsley   J. H. O'Connor   J. Cream   E. J. Forrest (Capt.)

Half-backs:
W. S. Browne   B. Tuke

LEFT.   RIGHT.

Three-quarter-backs:
H. Wells   L. H. Gwynne   S. Lee   W. Gardiner

Back:
W. Sparrow

Touch Judges: W. Cail and R. Garrett.   *Referee:* W. M. Douglas.

On the occasion of Wales' visit to the Rectory Field in 1902, it was the turn of the Welsh to conquer, winning the match 9-8. At this time Blackheath had three players in the England side, while the club was captained by Reg Skrimshire, a classy Welsh rugby footballer.

Another leading Welsh player who turned out for Blackheath was Johnny 'Birdie' Partridge. Partridge, a Welsh international, had turned out for South Africa while stationed there with the Army. His military commitments meant that the number of games he could play for his club sides was limited. While travelling back from a West of Scotland *v.* Blackheath fixture in 1906 he came up with the idea of forming an Army Rugby Union.

Alongside Partridge on his journey back from the West of Scotland was another serving soldier, W.S.O. Craven. Both men were junior officers at the time. Craven went on to reach the rank of Lt-Col in the Army. A strong forward and a great Blackheath man, he also became the club's secretary.

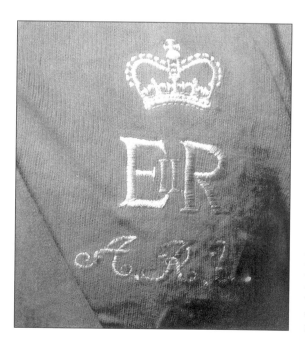

The idea of the Army Rugby Union was endorsed by the military and, in recognition of the role of Blackheath men in its establishment, the Rectory Field became the home ground of the Army in London. Blackheath's links with the Army have remained strong and the Army still play fixtures against the club on an annual basis.

From this 1907 Army side, Stevens, Begbie, Huntingford, Rogers, Hill and Partridge are all Blackheath players. Hill went on to be a Brigadier-General and president of the RFU.

Brig. H.L. Glyn Hughes, C.B.E., D.S.O., M.C., Q.H.P. (1892 – 1973), President of Blackheath 1930 – 55. President of the Barbarians 1955 – 73.

Brigadier Hugh Glyn Hughes was another military man who had a great impact on Blackheath as well as being a hard-working servant of rugby in general. In 1937, after a circular from the RFU had suggested that rough play should be curtailed on the rugby pitch, Hughes replied that the game had never been healthier.

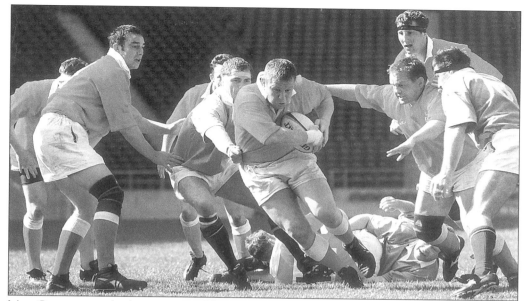

Matt Stewart was the last serving soldier to play regularly for Blackheath when he was part of their promotion-winning side of 1994/95. He also played the following year before moving to Northampton and winning international recognition with Scotland. He is seen here, ball in hand, playing for the Army.

Leon White was also on Blackheath's books while serving in the Army in 1995, but failed to make an impression. In the summer of 1995 he paid £200 to leave the Army, so that he could concentrate more on rugby. Here he is seen on the right of the picture watching Dom Walton (6) and Mick Harris compete for the ball.

The Rectory Field was also heavily used for Kent County games. In this picture of the 1920s you can clearly see the double-tier stand in the background. With no lifting in the line-out, players failed to get much height (although the Kent player with the twelve shirt appears to be pushing his team mate upwards).

In this picture of indeterminate age, the great W.G. Grace (centre with armband) poses with two sides outside the pavilion at Blackheath. From the early days to the present the pitch has been much-admired by cricketers.

In 1901 Scotland visited the Rectory Field to play England in front of 18,000 people. The two sides had won 27 games each before this fixture. On this occasion the Scots ended triumphant, winning by three goals and a try to one try.

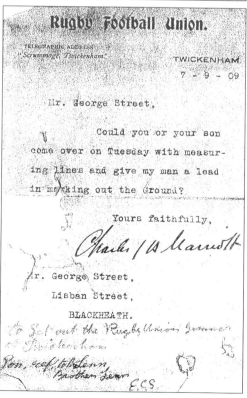

In 1909 the RFU finally moved out of the Rectory Field, establishing their own ground at Twickenham. George Street was requested by Charles Marriott, another former Blackheath player and by now secretary of the RFU, to help with the marking out of the pitch. George's son Len had already worked on the construction of the new pitch.

With the Rectory Field remaining an important venue in Kent rugby, the local side won the County Championship in 1927. They beat Leicester 22-2 with six Blackheath men in the side, plus former Blackheath man J.C. Hubbard, who was by then with Harlequins. Seated at the front on the right is Johnny Kemp, who played 250 first team games for Blackheath, a record for the club until well after the Second World War. When the Kent County Committee first introduced a Challenge Cup in 1890 for Kent sides, Blackheath's first XV was excluded on the basis that is was too strong for the competition. A Blackheath side entered in 1891/92 and won it, but again withdrew in subsequent years, even the second string proving to strong for the Kent sides to compete against.

Although the Rectory Field is no longer as important as it once was, it remains a historical ground. In 1981 when a game between past internationals was played between England and Wales to mark the centenary of the first England v. Wales game, four Blackheath men were down to play for England and one for Wales.

BLACKHEATH FOOTBALL CLUB

THE RECTORY FIELD BLACKHEATH

OFFICIAL PROGRAMME SEASON 1980/81

Founded 1858

COMMEMORATIVE MATCH
between Past International Players
E N G L A N D vs. W A L E S
to celebrate the Centenary of the first Rugby International
on Blackheath in February 1881
SATURDAY, 14th FEBRUARY, 1981
Kick Off 11.30 a.m.
BLACKHEATH vs. RICHMOND. Kick Off 2.30 p.m.

THE SWISS LIFE
WOMEN'S INTERNATIONAL

ENGLAND
v
SCOTLAND

&
ENGLAND A
v
SCOTLAND A

AT BLACKHEATH RFC
RECTORY FIELD

SUNDAY 26TH JANUARY 1997

KICK-OFF AT 12.00 NOON
& 2.00 PM

More recently the Rectory Field has played host to international women's rugby. The first ever game between England and Scotland at full level was played in 1997 on the site of the original pitch by the Princess of Wales pub. Sadly there were no Blackheath players in any of the four teams that started, although Rebecca Carlton was on the bench for England A.

47

Blackheath's standing in world rugby is clearly not what it was. This collage of rugger personalities produced in the 1920s contains no less than nine people associated with Blackheath, reflecting the importance of the club in the game.

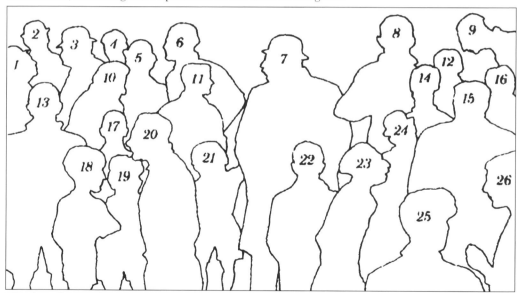

This key shows which of the great names were depicted by the artist: 1) G. Rowland Hill 2) Lt Col. W.S.D. Craven 3) C.J.B. Marriot 4) J. Daniell 5) E. Temple Gurdon 6) S.W. Harris 7) Major B.C. Hartley 8) H.C. Harrison 9) E. Loudoun Shand 10) F.C. Potter Irwin 11) V.R. Price 12) C.A. Kershaw 13) B.S. Cumberlege 14) A.T. Voyce 15) J. Birkett 16) G.B. Crole 17) A. Bates 18) C.N. Lowe 19) C. Lewis 20) W.W. Wakefield 21) H. Coverdale 22) R.A. Lloyd 23) W.J.A. Davies 24) A.D. Stoop 25) C.H. Pillman 26) J.E. Greenwood.

Four

Barbarians and the
Touring Tradition

The first real touring rugby side of any significance was the 1888 British side that went to Australasia. The original captain, R.L. Seddon, was killed in a swimming accident. His place was taken by Blackheath man Andrew Stoddart, who was the star of the tour. Stoddart is pictured second from the left in the back row.

A team mate of Stoddart's at Blackheath was 'Tottie' Carpmael, a tough-playing forward who was also a keen tourist. Carpmael was a great organiser who decided that because sides had trouble getting players together for bank holiday tours, it would be a good idea to have select teams to do so. His idea spawned the world-famous Barbarians in 1890.

Carpmael continued his involvement in Blackheath and was a great servant of the club. To this day The Club has two descendants of Percy Carpmael associated with it – Robert is a player with the amateur section and J.W.M. Carpmael is a non-playing member. Percy himself was a great Corinthian sportsman who also played football for the Corinthian Casuals.

The first Barbarians tour was organised for Christmas 1890. The name 'Barbarians' had been selected to indicate that the club would be an attacking force and, like the tribe of that name which operated in pre-Christian Germany, had no permanent home. A further reflection of the club's ethos was the skull and cross bone badge used on that tour. The badge was dropped after just the one tour, but the club remains homeless and continues its reputation for attacking rugby. The honour of playing for the Barbarians is only bettered by an international call-up and all the world's most famous players have turned out for the side. It was thought that the advent of professional rugby would bring about the Barbarians' demise, but they continue to put out first-class sides, raising money for charity.

One of the most prestigious touring sides to play at the Rectory Field was the New Zealand Maoris. Over 10,000 people packed the Rectory Field on 20 November 1926 to see the Maoris perform their 'weird haka'. The tourists had already defeated Cardiff and Swansea on their tour, so even a strong Blackheath side was not expected to win.

Both sides were introduced to the Prince of Wales before the fixture and in swirling winds Blackheath put up a useful display. Only the sure and solid tackling of the Maoris kept them at bay, the tourists eventually winning 9-5.

The successful side of 1927 made their Easter tour to the West Country. The season's successes included a cap for C.C. Bishop and triumph in the Middlesex Sevens. The top tryscorer had been Wynne, while the side also included such notables as England internationals W.E. Pratten and A.T. Young. Johnny Kemp went on this three-match tour with 249 Blackheath games to his credit, but did not play at all. Touring has always been an important part of clubs like Blackheath. In the interwar period the West Country was a favoured touring destination, the North East and Wales also featuring heavily as places Club visited, usually around Easter time. Sadly, with the advent of league tables, these trips are now normally only undertaken by junior sides rather than the first XV.

Racing Club of Paris was a popular opponent for Blackheath. In November 1928 the French side beat Blackheath 15-14 in Paris and when the return game was played on Boxing Day 1928 the French again won by a single point, this time 14-13. In this action shot H.A. Clayton-Greene is pictured failing to convert a Blackheath try during the second fixture.

Another favourite place for tours had been Germany. Frankfurt had been the first ever German side to come to England when they played Blackheath in 1894. The following year Blackheath went to Frankfurt. When the fixture pictured here was played on Boxing Day 1931 against Hanover, it was the first time a German side had visited Blackheath in twenty years. The difference in class was easy to tell, Blackheath winning the game 34-4.

After the Second World War Blackheath eventually re-established their traditional Boxing Day fixtures with Racing Club of Paris. In 1949 The Club were grateful of victory against the French: their domestic season had been going badly, the side reaching 22 October before recording a win.

After 1951 the Boxing Day games with Racing Club had been suspended due to the expense of travelling. Blackheath continued to keep up friendships abroad, however. In 1953 when they played Rugby Club Rouen of France the absence of club stalwart Peter Piper was so noticeable that the French sent a letter back saying how they missed him.

Blackheath's centenary year was regarded as being 1958/59, with many special events and games taking place throughout the season. Actress Milli Vitale added a little glamour to the fixture against a touring side from Milan, posing for a picture with Club skipper John Williamson and his Italian counterpart. Williamson was a devoted servant of Blackheath, making over 270 appearances before his retirement. He continued his association with the club and can still be found at the Rectory Field on match days.

The 1966 tour of East Africa came on the back of a relatively successful season for Blackheath. Just thirteen defeats had been registered in the campaign before twenty-four players embarked on a tour that saw them win nine from nine. Peter Bell is on the extreme left of the picture and the last Blackheath player on the right is Simon Clarke. Both men played for England that season. The ball carrier is Alan Hunt, with Paddy Mahon in attendance. Prior to the Second World War, and immediately after, tours had been short trips to other parts of Britain, or Europe, but with world-wide travel opening up Blackheath took the opportunity to visit more exotic places for greater lengths of time. Added to the usual itinerary of rugby and socialising was the pleasure of holiday-style tours taking in local culture.

Touring wasn't always about hard work. By the time that the club went to Nairobi in 1979, Merit Tables had been introduced, it now being the era of competitive rugby. However, that did not stop rugby players enjoying themselves. Tours were as much a holiday as a set of rugby fixtures, as displayed here by Jack Montgomery.

On the same tour, former skipper John Williamson finds all the excitement a little too much!

In 1980 Frankfurt invited Blackheath's veterans side over to help them celebrate their centenary. Frankfurt had long been off of the first fifteen's fixture card, but history remains a strong pull in Rugby Union. The German side had been so impressed with Blackheath on their first meeting that they had changed their strip to black and red hoops.

**Internationales
Rugby- und Hockey-Turnier**
100 Jahre Sport-Club „Frankfurt 1880 e. V."
Pfingsten 1980

The Golden Oldies that went out to Germany that year decided to lower the age of requirement to play for the side. The team shown here are part of their 'Golden Oldies Junior Colts' – all players being over the age of thirty, but not as old as the established Golden Oldies side.

Another club that holds Blackheath in high regard is the New Zealand outfit Christchurch. Like Frankfurt they adopted the back and red hoops in honour of Club, and also invited Blackheath over to celebrate their 125th anniversary in 1988.

That 1988 tour was taken with a view to developing the first team squad, but it also retained much that is traditional about rugby tours, the Golden Oldies side joining the first team squad down under. Here first team skipper Doug Hursey, at 6'8', is shown with Golden Oldie Rick Whiteman. Note that after training the first team player is holding beer cans, while the 5'11' Whiteman has a soft drinks can.

In 1991 the first team tour took the players to Australia. It was the year of the second rugby World Cup and attitudes to training were becoming more professional, even if players were still not being paid a regular wage. The first team squad seem to have the best of both worlds here, training hard on a sunny Australian beach.

One of Blackheath's keenest tourists has been Bobby Howe, seen here in Australia in 1991. Howe played over 300 games as a hooker for Blackheath, as well as representing England at under-23 level. His rugby tours have taken him to Spain, Portugal, Germany, Holland, Italy, USA, Canada, Papua New Guinea and Australia.

One of the most significant tours ever embarked on by Blackheath was the one that took them to South Africa in 1993. This was the first time that a British rugby side had gone into a South African township since the sporting boycott on South Africa had been lifted.

The tourists were immediately welcomed as heroes by the young people of the townships. Frank McCarthy, the club's chairman, is pictured here being mobbed by autograph hunters. Frank, himself a former second row player for the club, was instrumental in using his business connections to organise the tour.

Part of the tour itinerary included Blackheath players instructing young rugby players from the township of Zwide. This was seen as a fun and worthwhile thing by the players who threw themselves into the task, making many friends for Blackheath Rugby Club in the process. Fly half Sam Howard (left) and prop Terry Hodson are shown here watching as a young player heads for the tackle bag.

Zwide United were so impressed by Blackheath that they became the latest in a line of clubs to adopt the Blackheath colours of red and black. Their mini team became known as Blackheath South Africa. Back home in England, Blackheath people made huge efforts to collect kit to send out to their new-found African friends. Team secretary Ron Bailey is seen here with bags full of boots and kit waiting to be sent out to Zwide at the expense of Webster Bennett Ltd, a company owned by Club's Iain Exeter.

Blackheath's fall from grace has meant that recently there has been few players from the club representing England or the Barbarians. Mick Harris was finally selected to play for the Baa-baas in 1997 in Italy. Note the continuing tradition of players wearing the socks and shorts of their parent club.

Tonga became the first international side to play at the Rectory Field for many decades when they came to play Blackheath in 1997. The Tongan players were hosted in the traditional rugby fashion and taken to the Princess of Wales pub, a bar still regularly frequented by Club players. The game ended in a 20-20 draw.

Five
The World's Premier Club

When Club first introduced membership cards they could easily be slipped into the pocket. The 1972/73 version was the first to carry the club badge and when the 'red book' became the 'blue book' in 1995/96 it caused great concern to older, more traditionally-minded members of the club. In any event, membership of Blackheath, which in 1995 cost £40, has always been valued.

The oldest surviving club fixture in the world is that between Blackheath and nearby rivals Richmond. Richmond played a twenty-five-a-side match against Blackheath in January 1864, having previously been the first club to play a game under the rules of the Football Association. They preferred Blackheath rules, and opted not to join the FA. The game illustrated here was played in 1882, Blackheath winning by one try to nil. Richmond and Blackheath remained great friends and rivals from then on. Both sides slipped from the top rung of English rugby, even to the extent of sharing a season in National Division Three. Sadly, Richmond, like London Scottish, fell foul of professional rugby at the end of the 1998/99 season. Nevertheless, the club's amateur section continues, with the Richmond/Blackheath fixture continuing to hold a special place in the fixture list.

The first ever Anglo-Welsh fixture took place in Newport when Blackheath crushed their hosts by 4 goals and 9 tries to nil in November 1879. Newport were easily the best side in Wales at the time. By the time Club entertained Newport in March 1883, the team looked like a who's who of English rugby. Stokes became president of the RFU, while Marriott was for many years the RFU's secretary. Arthur Budd founded the London Referees' Society. The club's top try-getter at this time was W.N. Bolton. The fixture against Newport remained important throughout Club's history. Even later generations, with players such as Mick Skinner, revelled in the uncompromising rugby that was played out in these cross-border fixtures. The advent of league tables meant that the Newport fixture was suspended, but recently it has been reinstated as a pre-season friendly.

While the Stokes brothers put so much effort into establishing Blackheath and the game of rugby, by the time Andrew Stoddart joined the club the game was already a major attraction. Stoddart was a vastly talented sportsman who succeeded W.G. Grace in captaining the English cricket team. He was also an able hockey player.

Stoddart was an England player from 1886 until 1893, captaining the national side from 1889 to 1891 He was an internationally recognised player, who was once referred to by a team mate as 'The Much Paragraphed and Photographed One'.

While Blackheath were capable of drawing players from far and wide to wear the famous red and black hoops, they still recruited players from the Proprietary School. Johnny Fegan was a former Blackheath schoolboy who joined the team and went on to play for England, gaining three international caps in 1895. The following year he turned out for the school Old Boys in a fixture against Blackheath, the Old Boys winning 26-0!

The original rules of rugby counted a goal as being far more important than a try – tries simply gave a team the right to try and kick at goal – and a high percentage of kicks were missed. In this picture of Blackheath finally scoring a goal against Kensington note the high temporary stand along the side of the pitch.

Membership of rugby clubs has always been treated with significance. In the late 1890s members were given leather badges to be worn. Later, membership and fixture books were issued, but they became too bulky with the inclusion of fixtures ranging from under-7s to the veterans side. Currently, life members are awarded a specially struck enamel badge.

Familiar Football Faces.

No. XV.—C. H. PILLMAN, Blackhcath.

The first occasion on which my attention was directed to C. H. Pillman, the Blackheath forward, was under singular conditions. Kent were playing East Midlands, at Bedford, and before the start two well-known judges of the game approached me, each with a different piece of advice.

"You'll see to-day one of the worst type of forwards," said one. "Pillman, of Blackheath, does not push an ounce. I do not understand why Kent encourage him!"

Quoth the other: "You might keep an eye on that black-haired young fellow with his hair parted in the centre. He's a winger, but a jolly fine one. You'll like him!"

I made up my mind to watch for myself. Before long it was patent to me that this young Blackheath forward was a genius. It is true he lay on the verge of the scrummage, but he was waiting until the ball had been heeled out by his opponents. Then he was down on it like a shot. He did not always concede most licence, and was once or twice off-side, but repeatedly he broke away with fine dribbles, or again he dashed across the pitch to hold an opponent. There was little doubt about the utility of C. H. Pillman. The national selectors were of the same opinion.

When the English team to play the North, at Birkenhead Park, was chosen, Pillman was included, and he gave a very fine exhibition in the mud. He was one of the first men chosen for the second trial, England v. the South, at Twickenham, but influenza kept him out of the side, and in the Rest XV. against England he had on January 8 to work anew for distinction. He was the handiest forward on the field, just as a week later he was the bane of Dicky Owen and the Welsh backs generally. The Welsh match was a triumph for two men, C. H. Pillman and for Dai Gent. The little half-back was splendid; the forward was the spoiler-in-chief. Thus he was early picked to play against Ireland, at Twickenham, next Saturday, and only mishap can keep him out of other engagements. Such is the story of the development of Pillman.

This tall, clean-limbed man, who learned his football under the eye of Mr. R. L. Aston, at Tonbridge School, is the most notable forward of the day. Before a match his well-groomed appearance may not suggest the demon forward; but when a few scrummages have taken place, when his blood is up, and when his long hair half hides his features, there is a difference. Pillman has become as one of those weird figures which we associate with the player of American football. He stops at nothing; and he never gives in. He may not push, but he can be forgiven that lack of energy, because of his very zeal and his great effect in the open.

W. L. S.

EN PASSANT.

POEMS ON PLAYERS.

C. H. PILLMAN, Blackheath.

The forwards are packing,
No energy lacking,
All bent on attacking
The opposite line:
Heads down, they are pushing,
And shoving, and crushing,
And striving, and rushing
With energy fine.

See! up the scrum's breaking,
One pack the ball taking
The ball along, aching
For glory and tries;
My! who's that careering,
Nor flinching, nor veering,
But splendidly steering
His way to the prize?

That, gentles, is Pillman,
A forward of skill, man,
Whose doings would fill, man,
A jolly big book;
Impetuous? Very,
Yet fiercely merry—
He might hail from Derry,
But Blackheath's his nook.

On dribbles relying,
He's ever outvieing
His fellows, and flying,
The ball at his toe;
His style's of the old days—
The glorious, bold days—
The great, good-as-gold days
We once used to know.

Cherry Pillman, who was educated at Tonbridge School, was probably the most famous rugby player of the period before the First World War. He learnt his rugby at school under another great Blackheath man, Randolph Aston, and became the arch exponent of the new 'wing forward' position. Pillman would break from the scrum very quickly to set upon the opposition's ball carrier in midfield, thus 'spoiling' their game. It was a tactic that many traditionalists objected to and more recently the rules were changed to ensure the flanker remains bound to the scrum until the ball is out.

Pillman joined Blackheath from school in 1908. In that first season he played every position except full-back. By the end of the following campaign he was an England international and in 1910 he toured South Africa with the British side. He completely dominated the tour, scoring an amazing 65 points. In the final game of the tour, an 8-3 British win, he set up both tries and converted one of them while playing at fly-half. This picture shows the twenty year old Pillman on the South African tour.

Pillman played 18 times for England before breaking a leg in an international game. He continued to give good service to Blackheath after the war, both on the field and in the committee room. An extremely exciting and skilful player, he had changed the shape of rugby forever. His brother, Robert, was also a useful Blackheath player who collected an international cap before the outbreak of World War One. Sadly, Robert was killed in action during the conflict.

Fixtures against Welsh sides have always drawn great interest. Before this fixture of 1911, Club had not beaten Cardiff since 1895. They failed here again, drawing the game 3-3 in front of 5,000 fans. Pillman, Le Stone, Coverdale and Pym, all shown here, were international players.

The side that completed the 1913/14 season was unquestionably the best in the land. They won 21 games and lost just 5. Six of the players pictured here were internationals. Sadly, three of them were among the sixty-one Club members killed in the hostilities. From left to right, back row: B. Hartley, D. De Villiers, Q. King, C. Hemmerde. Middle row: V. Cunis, J. Watson, H. Hughes, A. Sykes, R. Juckes, C. Bates, H. Walker. Front row: W. Craven, C. Pillman, H. Coverdale, G. Smith, R. Pillman. Seated on step: S. Cook, A. Horan. Inset: F. Le Stone.

Following the war Blackheath had an even stronger side than before the conflict. With Cherry Pillman taking over as captain, their 1919/20 season saw them win 23 games, losing just 2 (both against Newport). South African giant Stanley Harris scored a club record 31 tries in the season, whilst Cyril Lowe, a former Dulwich School pupil, scored 22. Crowds came in their thousands to witness the supreme play of Lowe, Harris and Pillman. A total of eight Blackheath players received international call-ups. From left to right, back row: C. Merriam, C. Hemmerde, F. Hawes, G. Hubbard. Middle row: F. Gwynne, H.R. Prior, F. Spriggs, A.P.B. Roberts, H. Hughes, A. Aslett, MeUish, S. Harris, E.C. Kinghorn. Front row: W. Craven, B. Cumberlege, C. Pillman, H. Coverdale, F. Le Stone. Seated on step: A. Horan, C. Lowe.

By 1922 Blackheath were still big crowd-pullers, with an entertaining style of play. They were not, however, as successful, due in part to the fact that many of their players were only available for some of the season. In this, the first ever action picture used by the local paper, they are taking on London Scottish. The Blackheath player watching from the edge of the scrum is Cyril Lowe.

Lionel Bailey tussles for the ball in front of a good Rectory Field crowd, c. 1925. Success comes and goes for all sports sides, but tradition is an important thing to be maintained. Bailey was the father of C.B. Bailey, who played for the club in the 1950s. In C.B.'s side were Bill Tucker, Jon Bishop, S. Arnold and R. Berkeley – all sons of Blackheath players.

Rugby was still a popular game in the 1920s and '30s, with Blackheath remaining as one of the country's top clubs. Many of their players were immortalised on cigarette cards as a marketing device for tobacco companies. Carl Aarvold joined Blackheath in 1928, gaining his first international cap after signing for the club.

Arthur Young was another very popular England international who played for Blackheath in the 1920s. Standing just 5' 5' tall he was a dashing scrum half who, like Pillman, owed his early training to Randolph Aston at Tonbridge School. A masterful reader of the game, he was a Cambridge Blue whose appearances were only kept down by his study and military commitments.

Things do not always go right, even for the best of superstars. In this picture it is the turn of Stanley Cook to receive the assistance of Charlie Street in putting on a new pair of shorts, his original pair being torn on this occasion in around 1925. The players in the huddle are forwards, the shirt numbering system being almost the reverse of that which is used today.

Anglo-Welsh fixtures have always been an important part of the rugby calendar, especially the one between Blackheath and Newport. When the two sides met at the Rectory Field in 1926, Newport had not lost against the Londoners for twenty years. Despite the fact that the Welsh side contained ten internationals, Blackheath deservedly won the game 11-6. Speedy winger Dennis Morris is shown collaring his man.

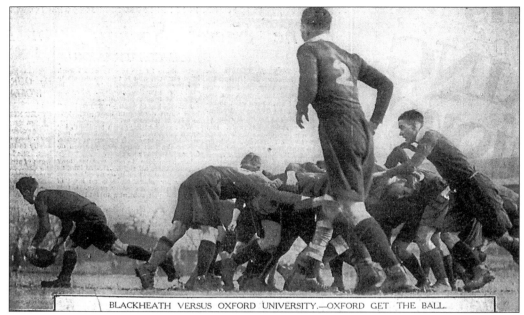

BLACKHEATH VERSUS OXFORD UNIVERSITY.—OXFORD GET THE BALL.

Dennis Morris, wearing number two, was one of the most successful players on Blackheath's books that never got to play for England. He represented Sussex and later Leicestershire and many thought his speed would be an asset to the national side. The number two shirt denotes his position as a winger.

Another great player that never quite made it to the England side was Johnny Kemp. Kemp turned out 250 times for Blackheath (then a record). He completed the 250 while the club secretary in 1936 on tour to the West Country, which was ironic as three years previously he had gone on the same tour, but was not picked to play in any of the games.

The 1932/33 team, led by Carl Aarvold, was up against strong opposition, both on the pitch and as local crowd pullers. Catford dog track had just opened, pulling in 30,000 for its first meeting and Charlton Athletic were fancied for promotion. Despite this, Aarvold's side had a spectacular season. They drew over 5,000 to some of their home games and although they did, in fact, lose 4 games, they won 30 and were recognised as the best team in Britain at the time.

For ten years Blackheath's strength in depth was indicated by their ability to put out an 'Extra "A" Fifteen'. This side regularly beat other club's first choice sides and often contained players with international experience – even the great Stanley Harris played for it. Nevertheless, the habit of putting out two first teams was never fully accepted as it lead to unnecessary defeats at times. The practise was ceased at the start of the 1934/35 season.

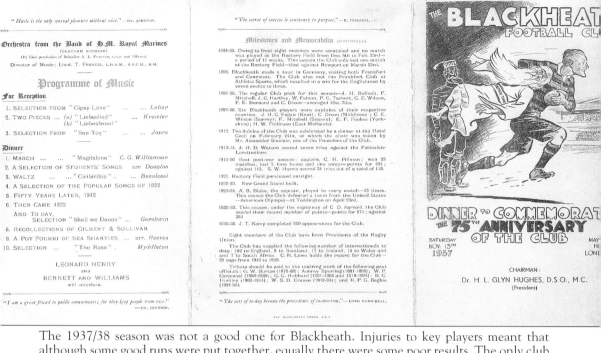

The 1937/38 season was not a good one for Blackheath. Injuries to key players meant that although some good runs were put together, equally there were some poor results. The only club player to make it into the national side was full-back G. Parker.

The disappointments on the pitch did not stop Club from celebrating their seventy-fifth anniversary, however. A grand event was laid on at the Mayfair Hotel in central London.

BLACKHEATH WIN

NORTHERN'S GOOD SHOWING

BRISTOL BEAT LEICESTER

NARROW VICTORY FOR WATERLOO

BY OUR OWN CORRESPONDENTS

BLACKHEATH 18 pts.   NORTHERN 8

Instead of going on tour this Easter Blackheath have stayed at home, and they had a large gathering yesterday to watch Northern, from Newcastle, pay their first visit to the Rectory Field. And a grand game it was in the sunshine, with the ball always in the open. Blackheath won yet again by three goals and a try to a goal and a penalty goal, but there was nothing like that difference between the teams.

Blackheath, it is true, were without several of their key men, notably W. O. Chadwick, the hooker, and G. A. Walker at stand-off half, but they had all the ball for the first twenty minutes or so, and there was no inkling of the hair-raising escapes their line was to suffer. Northern, a nicely balanced side, scrummaged to such good purpose in the 3-4-1 formation that they did nearly all the heeling in the second half; ironically enough, it was then that Blackheath scored fifteen of their points, though, with the referee unsighted, there was a good deal of doubt about their last try.

It said much for the reserves of Blackheath that their forwards could play with such power in the loose, where men like D. T. Kemp, L. S. Bailey, E. G. Cooper, and F. J. L. Cary really won the match. Northern had players after their own heart in W. F. Blackadder, who got his cap for Scotland at Twickenham last year, and M. Cranfield. Northern's strategist was clearly T. A. Dickinson, the right-centre, who liked to use the short punt ahead—he often had S. I. Howard-Jones, at full-back, fumbling badly—and scored all their points. J. S. Bartlett, too, was a dangerous left wing, and he all but scored two tries.

At once it was evident that Northern were made of sterner stuff than Headingley the previous week. They might have scored in the first minute when Howard-Jones lost the ball behind his line, but that player made up for the shock soon afterwards when he dashed up-field, took a return pass from J. S. Moll, and sent J. D. Carmichael over in the corner.

A measured drop at goal from half-way by Howard-Jones was wide, and then Northern were constantly attacking. Always Blackheath's defence was too good, specially the tackling of Moll and the fast legs of W. P. Barton, who once headed off A. D. Forster, the Northern stand-off, in a stirring race for the goal posts.

Northern came down fiercely at the start of the second half, and Bartlett was caught in the nick of time when J. G. W. Davies and Howard-Jones converged on him. It was just a yard of finishing speed that Northern lacked most, for several times they were clean through and then overtaken.

Blackheath scored a fine try against the run of the game from an interception by Davies, which ended in J. L. Chambers, a fine scrummage half-back, veering away between the posts. That, too, was where Moll grounded the ball, after a long zig-zagging run with R. Stringfellow, the full-back, at his elusive heels; and making goals of these tries was easy for Howard-Jones.

By that time Dickinson, a curiously unpolished but most effective kick, had scored a penalty goal from 45 yards for Northern. After missing another from shorter range, he ran through the entire defence; the last push from a Blackheath arm almost sent him hurtling between the posts, and he converted his own try.

Northern were decidedly the attacking side now against a cool and deliberate defence. Anything might have happened in the last ten minutes had not R. E. Lauder, a capable stand-off player, set up a clever run on the blind side that he himself finished off from Kemp and Cary, though he seemed to knock-on before he grounded the ball. Howard-Jones's goal kick hit the far post and glanced the right way—the last instance of Blackheath's luck of the bounce.

By the time that the Second World War broke out, Blackheath were once again regarded as a top side. They had a poor start to the 1938/39 season but a strong finish indicated they were ready to return once more to the top of the game. However, when war broke out Club indicated that because their players had scattered around various army camps they would not, unlike many other sides, even attempt to play scratch games during hostilities.

Six

Struggling with the New Order

Blackheath did not acquire a proper crest for themselves until the 1950s. Prior to that if a crest was to be used it was the old Proprietary School badge. Even after the new badge was adopted it was not used on the playing shirts until the 1970s.

Following the Second World War, Blackheath's Rectory Field ground was not ready for the start of the 1945/46 season. Furthermore, the club did not have the playing resources to put out a regular side. For that first campaign they pooled their resources with West London rivals, Richmond, playing their early games at the Athletic Ground.

Even with a joint side the two clubs were weak. They lost the opening game 17-5 against a youthful Northampton and when the joint club made their first appearance of the season at the Rectory Field, on 8 December 1945, they lost 18-6 against St Mary's Hospital.

A one minute silence will be observed by the Teams before the commencement of play in memory of their fellow club members who fell in the War.

Official Programme 3d.

RUGBY FOOTBALL

Richmond Athletic Ground

E. de LISSA, Secretary.

Richmond & Blackheath

versus

NORTHAMPTON

ON

Saturday, September 22nd, 1945

Kick-off 3.15 p.m.

J. H. Broad & Co., Ltd., Printers, 8, King Street, Richmond, Surrey.

FIXTURE LIST 1945-46.

KICK-OFF p.m.			
3. 0	Sat.	Sept. 15	Trials
3.15	Sat.	Sept. 22	Richmond & Blackheath v Northampton
3.15	Sat.	Sept. 29	London Scottish v London Irish
3.15	Sat.	Oct. 6	London Scottish v Harlequins
3. 0	Sat.	Oct. 13	Richmond & Blackheath v Swansea
3. 0	Sat.	Oct. 20	London Scottish v R.A.A.F.
2.45	Sat.	Oct. 27	London Scottish v Bedford
2.45	Sat.	Nov. 3	London Scottish v Cambridge University
2.45	Sat.	Nov. 10	
2.30	Sat.	Nov. 17	Richmond & Blackheath v London Scottish
2.30	Sat.	Nov. 24	
2.30	Sat.	Dec. 1	Richmond & Blackheath v Cardiff
			London Scottish v Wasps
2.30	Sat.	Dec. 8	Richmond & Blackheath v St. Mary's Hospital (at Blackheath)
2.30	Sat.	Dec. 15	London Scottish v Old Alleynians
2.30	Sat.	Dec. 22	Richmond & Blackheath v Harlequins
2.30	Wed.	Dec. 26	Richmond & Blackheath v Wasps
2.30	Sat.	Dec. 29	English Schools v Scottish Schools
1946.			
			London Scottish v Gloucester
2.30	Sat.	Jan. 5	Richmond & Blackheath v Guy's Hospital (at Blackheath)
2.30	Sat.	Jan. 12	London Scottish v Rosslyn Park
2.45	Sat.	Jan. 19	Richmond & Blackheath v Cambridge University
2.45	Sat.	Jan. 26	London Scottish v Oxford University
2.45	Sat.	Feb. 2	Richmond & Blackheath v Oxford University
2.45	Tues.	Feb. 5	Hospital Cup—Round 1
2.45	Thur.	Feb. 7	Hospital Cup—Round 1
3. 0	Sat.	Feb. 9	Richmond & Blackheath v London Scottish
2.45	Tues.	Feb. 12	Hospital Cup—Round 1
2.45	Thur.	Feb. 14	Hospital Cup—Round 2
3. 0	Sat.	Feb. 16	Richmond & Blackheath v Bristol
2.45	Tues.	Feb. 19	Hospital Cup—Round 2
2.45	Thur.	Feb. 21	Hospital Cup—Round 2
	Sat.	Feb. 23	NO MATCH
2.45	Tues.	Feb. 26	Hospital Cup—Round 2
3. 0	Sat.	Mar. 2	London Scottish v Richmond & Blackheath
2.45	Tues.	Mar. 5	Hospital Cup—Semi-Final
2.45	Thur.	Mar. 7	Hospital Cup—Semi-Final
3. 0	Sat.	Mar. 9	London Scottish v United Services
	Sat.	Mar. 16	NO MATCH
3. 0	Wed.	Mar. 20	Hospital Cup—Final
3.15	Sat.	Mar. 23	Richmond & Blackheath v United Services
2.30	Sat.	Mar. 30	London Scottish v Bath
2.45	Sat.	Mar. 30	Richmond & Blackheath v Coventry
3.15	Sat.	Apr. 6	
3. 0	Sat.	Apr. 13	United Hospitals—Seven-a-Side

TEAMS.

Richmond & Blackheath (Colours—Red, Black and Old Gold)			Northampton (Colours—Black, Green and Gold)
1 P. B. C. MOORE	Back		1 G. ADKINS
	Three-qrs		
2 J. A. MORGAN	RW.	LW.	2 R. O. PELL
3 R. FISHER	RC.	LC.	3 L. LONGLAND
4 A. L. WARR	LC.	RC.	6 L. CANNELL
5 G. A. RICHMOND	LW.	RW.	7 W. Y. WRIGHT
6 D. J. PIPER	Outside Half		8 J. M. PELL
7 J. PARSONS	Scrum Half		9 G. STIMPSON
8 G. J. RICHARDSON			10 A. P. BELL (Capt.)
9 G. A. SMITH			11 W. R. HAMP
10 R. BUCHANAN-ALLEN			12 D. F. WHITE
11 C. D. LABORDE (Capt.)	Forwards		13 F. JEFFCOATE
12 J. W. V. JENNENS			14 P. BRADBURY
14 G. A. PETERS			15 B. J. B. HAZEL
15 R. A. BETHEL			16 W. J. WILLIAMS
16 J. W. E. MARK			17 S. KITCHENER

Referee : - - Mr. G. WARDEN

By the start of the 1946/47 season the Rectory Field was in fine shape once again. One of the highlights of a poor season was when Charlton Athletic's FA Cup winning side took on Blackheath at cricket. Both sides had players capable of playing first class cricket if they had not chosen to play a winter sport instead.

The cricket match against Charlton was a benefit for the near-legendary groundsman Charlie Street. As can be seen from the family tree, even the women of the Street family were involved in working at the Rectory Field – Louisa Isobella Street pulled the first ever pint served at the new Rectory Field Pavilion!

Football Teams Play Cricket.

SYD JORDAN'S impressions of the match.

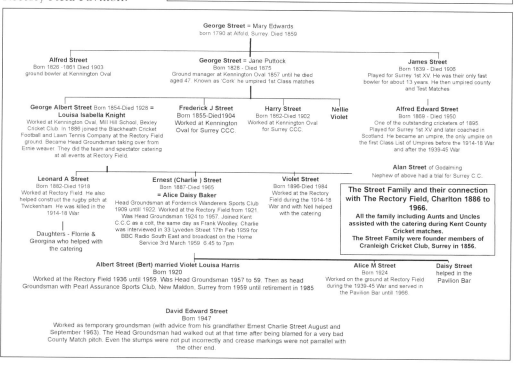

George Street = Mary Edwards
born 1790 at Alfold, Surrey. Died 1859

Alfred Street
Born 1826 -1861 Died 1903
ground bowler at Kennington Oval

George Street = Jane Puttock
Born 1828 - Died 1875
Ground manager at Kennington Oval 1857 until he died aged 47. Known as 'Cork' he umpired 1st Class matches

James Street
Born 1839 - Died 1906
Played for Surrey 1st XV. He was their only fast bowler for about 13 years. He then umpired county and Test Matches

George Albert Street Born 1854-Died 1928 =
Louisa Isabella Knight
Worked at Kennington Oval, Mill Hill School, Bexley Cricket Club. In 1886 joined the Blackheath Cricket Football and Lawn Tennis Company at the Rectory Field ground. Became Head Groundsman taking over from Ernie weaver. They did the team and spectator catering at all events at Rectory Field.

Frederick J Street
Born 1855-Died1904
Worked at Kennington Oval for Surrey CCC.

Harry Street
Born 1862-Died 1902
Worked at Kennington Oval for Surrey CCC.

Nellie Violet

Alfred Edward Street
Born 1869 - Died 1950
One of the outstanding cricketers of 1895. Played for Surrey 1st XV and later coached in Scotland. He became an umpire, the only umpire on the first Class List of Umpires before the 1914-18 War and after the 1939-45 War.

Alan Street of Godalming
Nephew of above had a trial for Surrey C.C.

Leonard A Street
Born 1882-Died 1918
Worked at Rectory Field. He also helped construct the rugby pitch at Twickenham. He was killed in the 1914-18 War.

Daughters - Florrie & Georgina who helped with the catering

Ernest (Charlie) Street
Born 1887-Died 1965
= Alice Daisy Baker
Head Groundsman at Forderrick Wanderers Sports Club 1909 untill 1922. Worked at the Rectory Field from 1921. Was Head Groundsman 1924 to 1957. Joined Kent C.C.C as a colt, the same day as Frank Woolley. Charlie was interviewed in 33 Lyveden Street 17th Feb 1959 for BBC Radio South East and broadcast on the Home Service 3rd March 1959 6.45 to 7pm

Violet Street
Born 1896-Died 1984
Worked at the Rectory Field during the 1914-18 War and with Nell helped with the catering

The Street Family and their connection with The Rectory Field, Charlton 1886 to 1966.
All the family including Aunts and Uncles assisted with the catering during Kent County Cricket matches.
The Street Family were founder members of Cranleigh Cricket Club, Surrey in 1856.

Albert Street (Bert) married Violet Louisa Harris
Born 1920
Worked at the Rectory Field 1936 until 1959. Was Head Groundsman 1957 to 59. Then as head Groundsman with Pearl Assurance Sports Club, New Maldon, Surrey from 1959 until retirement in 1985

Alice M Street
Born 1924
Worked on the ground at Rectory Field during the 1939-45 War and served in the Pavilion Bar untill 1966.

Daisy Street
helped in the Pavilion Bar

David Edward Street
Born 1947
Worked as temporary groundsman (with advice from his grandfather Ernest Charlie Street August and September 1963). The Head Groundsman had walked out at that time after being blamed for a very bad County Match pitch. Even the stumps were not put incorrectly and crease markings were not parrallel with the other end.

London Irish

R.F.C.

Programme

THE RECTORY FIELD,
BLACKHEATH

Price 3d.

From the start of the 1948 season, Blackheath had a range of tenants at the Rectory Field. London Irish moved in to play their first team fixtures there, while for a brief period Sunday football was played on the ground between teams from the Metropolitan Sunday League.

The Exiles tenancy lasted until 1959, by which time a great deal of friendship had developed. Note that the programme for Exile fixtures also advertises games played by Blackheath at the Rectory Field, rather than informing spectators of their own away games.

1951/52 FIXTURES
AT THE RECTORY FIELD

1951		1952	
Sept.	15 D. W. Swarbrick's XV v. A. M. Rees's XV	Jan.	6 L.I. v. Harlequins
	22 L.I. v. United Services		12 B. v. Harlequins
	29 B. v. Coventry		19 B. v. Penzance (11 a.m.)
Oct.	6 B. v. Birkenhead Park		26 B. v. Royal Navy
	13 L.I. v. Northampton	Feb.	2 L.I. v. Blackheath
	20 L.I. v. Middlesex Hosp.		16 L.I. v. Bath
	27 B. v. Llanelly		23 B. v. Newport
Nov.	3 B. v. London Welsh	Mar.	1 L.I. v. St. Mary's Hospital
	8 L.I. v. Oxford University		15 B. v. London Scottish
	17 L.I. v. Univ. Coll. Dublin		22 L.I. v. Aldershot Services
	19 L.I. v. Dublin University		29 L.I. v. Notts.
	24 L.I. v. Guys Hospital	April	5 B. v. Bristol
Dec.	1 B. v. Wasps		14 B. v. London Hospital
	8 L.I. v. London Welsh		
	15 B. v. Richmond		B. — Blackheath
	22 L.I. v. Blackheath		L.I. — London Irish
	26 B. v. Kent Old Boys		
	29 L.I. v. Rome Club, Societa Sportiva Roma		

LONDON IRISH v. ALDERSHOT SERVICES

Saturday, March 22, 1952

	LONDON IRISH				ALDERSHOT SERVICES
1	A. S. McKee	Full Back		1	Major A. F. Campbell
2	†C. S. Griffin	Three-Qtrs.		2	2/Lt. J. G. Lee
3	M. Powell			3	Spr. G. Browne
4	S. O. B. Pierce			4	Pte. G. A. Long
5	P. E. Whittaker			5	2/Lt. D. Bedford
6	*D. A. Orr	Half Backs		6	A. N. Other
7	D. A. Malone			7	A. N. Other
8	°T. S. McRoberts	Forwards		8	Lt. W. A. J. Summerskill
9	°H. D. Doherty			9	2/Lt. T. G. Barrett
10	A. G. Hill			10	Pte. A. Townsend
11	D. McSweeney			11	Pte. I. Zaidman
12	T. A. Gallagher			12	L/Cpl. L. H. Webb
13	T. G. Davis			13	Cap. A. Mc. L. Morrison
14	J. S. Ritchie			14	*Capt. H. I. A. Thompson
15	R. P. Bellingham			15	O/C. Paisley

REFEREE :- Mr. A. Stewart.

* Captain † International ° Blue

This fixture against London Irish in the 1960s was England international scrum-half Simon Clarke's last game for Blackheath (he is the player kicking the ball in the picture). Irish player Tony O'Riley was also making his last bow in this match.

FESTIVAL RUGBY FOOTBALL AT THE RECTORY FIELD BLACKHEATH ON SATURDAY, 15TH SEPTEMBER

AT 2.45 P.M.

1. SHORT GAME WITH RULES AND DRESS AS IN 1862.

AT 3.15 P.M.

2. D. W. SWARBRICK'S SIDE CONSISTING ENTIRELY OF INTERNATIONAL PLAYERS

AGAINST

A. M. REES' SIDE CONSISTING ALSO ENTIRELY OF INTERNATIONAL PLAYERS

Admission to Ground, 2/-   Children, 1/-
Stand 10/- & 7/6 (including Admission)   Rope Seats 6/- (including Admission)
Terraced Enclosure 2'6 (in addition to entrance)

STAND, and ROPE seats may be obtained after 15th August, on application to Alfred Mays, 74 Cornhill, E.C.3., or 26 Old Bond Street, W.1., or from Mr. M. A. Tallby, Rectory Field, Blackheath. No Refunds can be given.

Frequent trains from Charing Cross, London Bridge and Waterloo to Blackheath and/or Westcombe Park.
No. 55* Bus from Haymarket and Whitehall to Rectory Field or 701 or 702 Green Line from Hyde Park Corner and Victoria.

Club has always been aware of its position in the history of rugby, celebrating anniversaries as appropriate. In 1951, 8,000 people turned up at the Rectory Field to watch a game played in 1862 period costume to mark the 100th anniversary of the formal inception of the club.

In theory the 1954/55 side should have contained England and Army half-back pairing Hardy and Shuttleworth, but they missed many games as well as this photocall because of Army commitments. Full-back Neil Escourt gained an international cap in this season and was famous for his 'scissors' move. Many also felt Wally Gray to be the best winger in the country, but he never made it to international level.

On paper this 1965/66 side was a very strong one. It contained five internationals and a British Lion, yet the results were mixed. Skipper Simon Clarke had taken over the role from the successful Pat King, who left after internal wrangles. The addition of Tony Jorden, who was also a county cricketer for Essex, proved popular with supporters, however. From left to right, back row: M. Beckwith, P. Piper, J. Turner, C. Benstead, C. Hacking, M. Newson (personnel). Middle row: D. Kinsey, I. Exeter, W. Bending, M. Bulpitt, P. Burn, P. Thorne, G. Stringer, J. Williamson (manager). Front row: A. Hunt, A. Horton, S. Clarke, D. Stevens, B. Ostling, J. Mawbey. Seated: P. Mahon, T. Jorden. Peter Bell, the England pack-leader, is missing from the photograph.

This 1971/72 team is the last put out by Blackheath that contained a current England international, in this case Mike Bulpitt. This was the year that the RFU introduced competitive rugby in the form of the National Knock-out Cup. Club whipped Sidcup 30-3 in the first round before going down 12-4 to Harlequins. Note that the playing shirts still did not contain the club badge.

Ian Williamson, seen here in action for Kent in 1977, was a player of immense talent who skippered the club side. A reliable kicker of the dead ball, he had trials for England, but by this time it was difficult to achieve international recognition if playing for a club like Blackheath, who were struggling to make their mark.

In the 1981/82 season Blackheath introduced a new flanker into the side that played against London Scottish in the John Player Cup. Danny Vaughan, seen here supporting Mick Skinner in April 1982, was a local boxer who had turned to rugby. Teaming up with Skinner in Club's back row, Vaughan was a fiery player who went on to pick up the Player of the Year award twice, before injury cut short his career. The two back row men terrorised opposition defences, scoring many tries between them before Skinner's move to Harlequins. When he finished playing, Vaughan took up coaching positions at Blackheath, eventually becoming the first team's head coach. He left briefly to coach Westcombe Park in 1997/98, returning just 1½ seasons later.

Fly-half Nick Colyer arrived at the club in 1983, his career being ended by an eye-injury in 1988. Colyer was one of several players that could have advanced his career by moving from Blackheath, but stayed with the club out of loyalty. This picture shows him scoring a try against Sutton and Epsom in the 1984 John Player Cup match, won by Blackheath 40-6.

Paul Matthews, pictured here being sandwiched by London Scottish players in 1983, went on to coach Blackheath in 1989. His scientific approach to training brought some success to the club and in 1992 he issued an internal paper, called 'Crisis Point', outlining ways for the club to move forward. The main proposal that was adopted by the committee was that a director of rugby be appointed. The first man to take that position was Alan Davies. Matthews' work commitments meant that he did not stay at the club to see the benefits of his ideas. He went to Rosslyn Park before moving to Scotland.

During a disappointing period on the pitch (that lasted several decades), the clubhouse at Blackheath received little in the way of modernisation. The open side of the pitch cannot be built on by law, restricting the club's plans for development. This picture was taken before the extension was built on the front of the pavilion.

Inside the cosy clubhouse there is an amazing area of shirts, plaques and memorabilia to remind drinkers of the history of the world's oldest open rugby club. The shirts have been presented by club players that have gone on to gain representative honours.

During a long period when Blackheath were having little success on the pitch, one of their most famous sons, Mick Skinner, was bathing himself in glory as an international player of repute. Skinner had left Blackheath to play rugby at a higher level, but his heart remained with the South East London outfit, many of his shirts still adorning the club house wall.

After a successful spell with Harlequins, from where he played for England and the Lions, Skinner returned to his beloved Blackheath in 1992. Installed as skipper, he was to act as a beacon for the club. This picture shows his concentration during Club's 21-9 victory against London Welsh in the Pilkington Cup in 1993.

By the start of the 1993/94 season, with Danny Vaughan as coach, Club had little but memories and a small trophy cabinet to remind themselves of their once glorious past. The aim was straightforward – put Club back in the big time. Promotion just eluded the side that year, but the foundation was laid for the next, successful, campaign.

Full-back Stuart Burns was in the side that was put together to push Blackheath towards promotion in 1994/95. Burns, a Cambridge Blue, was an enigmatic player. Although on his day he was capable of playing at the highest level, injury problems and inconsistency sadly let him down.

Coach Danny Vaughan felt that the squad was a player or two short of what was required to gain promotion and retain a place in the higher division. Alex Codling, who later joined Richmond before moving on to Bedford, was considered a key acquisition in the bid for promotion.

Another player brought in mid-season was prop Paul Shadbolt. Shadbolt, a powerful ball-in-hand player helped lift the side immeasurably. 12-0 down at home to closest rivals, Bedford, Club fought back to a 12-12 draw that as-good-as secured promotion. The revival was sparked by a Shadbolt try.

By the time the last game of the season was played, down at Exeter, Club were already promoted. Victory was nevertheless secured, ensuring that the players felt entitled to their post-game celebrations.

Having gained promotion to Courage League Two, Blackheath consolidated well. They still had a young side who were eager to perform well for their club. Hooker Colin Ridgway, who gained the club Player of the Year award in 1997/98, joined First Division Harlequins from Blackheath.

Although newly promoted, Club were not taken lightly. Several of the players went on to join First Division sides when the team was broken up in 1997. Mick Friday (playing the ball) went on to Wasps, while Sam Howard (in the foreground) joined Bedford.

Now a professional sport, rugby had to do its best to attract sponsorship and media coverage. Blackheath used famous comedy duo Hale and Pace, both supporters of the club, to promote their new playing kit in 1995/96.

At the end of the 1995/96 season, veteran hooker Bobby Howe was voted squad Player of the Year, his award being presented by Cheryl Baker, formerly of pop band Bucks Fizz.

Former All-Black hooker Hika Reid joined Club's coaching staff in 1996. By the end of the season he had become Blackheath's first – and to date last – paid, full-time coach. Reid helped assemble a side that had quality throughout, but sadly rarely got the team to play to sum of its parts.

There had been high hopes for the 1996/97 season. Only two of the opening six games had ended in defeat, away wins being gained at Nottingham and London Scottish. Mick Harris and Mark Hanslip are shown here combining to fell Richmond's Scott Quinnell, whilst Rob McCorduck looks on.

Interest in rugby and Blackheath was such that a huge crowd turned out for a mid-week match when Club played Newcastle in April 1997. Even a strong Club side fell 72-10 against a star-studded Rob Andrew team.

Part of the proposed deal with New Zealand outfit Auckland Blues included legendary coach Graham Henry spending a short time at Blackheath. While Henry was involved in the coaching in 1997/98, Club beat London Scottish and West Hartlepool, who were both promoted, as well as giving Saracens a good game in the Tetley Bitter Cup.

The New Zealand connection looked to be paying off, on paper at least. John Gallagher and John Schuster were both well-known All-Blacks, while John Clarke was establishing himself as a Western Samoan scrum-half with an awesome reputation. In fact Schuster injured a shoulder and made few appearances for Blackheath and Gallagher had only one good season, while Clarke often appeared to be making a one-man stand against Club's opponents.

The number of changes to the team in 1997 were such that the programme editors felt that introductions were needed!

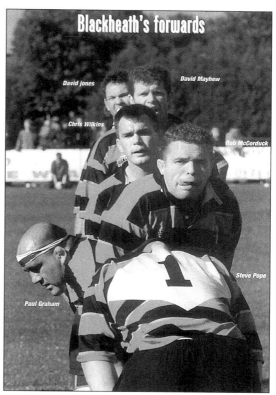

Blackheath's forwards

David jones
David Mayhew
Chris Wilkins
Rob McCorduck
Steve Pope
Paul Graham

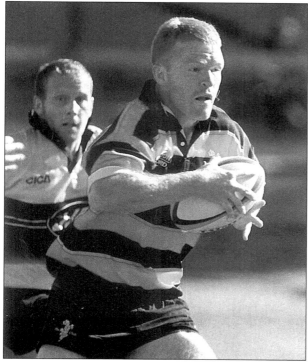

Former All-Black and Lewisham-born full-back John Gallagher was the club skipper for the second year in 1997/98. The side contained a number of players capable of First Division rugby, but underachieved as a unit. Gallagher left in the summer to become director of rugby at Harlequins.

Danny Vaughan returned to Club for the start of the 1998/99 season. Seen here on the left with Iain Exeter during his first stint as coach, Vaughan had the difficult task of leading a team that was re-adjusting back to semi-professional status after the experiment of professional rugby. He also had to weld together a team that was only gathered together as the season approached. An almost impossible task, Vaughan could not stop Club slipping down to Jewson's League One, the third division of English rugby.

John Clarke is seen here collecting another try against Fylde in 1998. In 1997 he scored a club record four tries against the northerners. On his return to Blackheath in December 1998 he scored another two against Bill Beaumount's former club. Dave Merlin is the player looking on.

On his return to Blackheath Vaughan appointed back row forward Chris Wilkins as club skipper. Wilkins, a former England A man had, while at Wasps, been considered a long term England prospect before a nasty neck injury forced his to reconsider his career pattern.

Clarke became the professional rugby club's first true hero. His ability to crunch through tackles won him the admiration of Club fans and his ability to lift the team around him nearly caused the side to climb clear of the inevitable drop from Premiership status at the end of 1998/99 season. His tally for that campaign was 11 tries from just 10 starts and 3 substitute appearances.

Seven

The Short Game –
Rugby Sevens

The game of rugby sevens was invented by the Scots as a money raising exercise, but is now a game played worldwide at the end of each season. The most prestigious sevens contest in England is that organised by Middlesex Rugby Union – the Russell Cargill Trophy.

SEVEN-A-SIDE RUGBY.

HARLEQUINS WIN THE FIRST TOURNAMENT.

If the size of the crowd at Twickenham on Saturday can be taken seriously, Seven-a-side Rugby has come to stay in England —in London, at any rate. There must have been nearly 15,000 people to watch the closing stages of the experimental tournament organized by the Middlesex County Union, and the Middlesex Hospital Reconstruction Fund, towards which the proceeds were devoted, must have benefited considerably.

A cup had been offered for competition, and this was won by the Harlequins, whose First VII., composed largely of international players, having steadily played themselves into something like the correct seven-a-side game, were altogether too much for St. Mary's Hospital in the final match. St. Mary's, however, had done their full share towards entertaining a crowd that might easily have been disappointed—and, in fact, were becoming so—by defeating the Old Merchant Taylors in one of two most exciting semi-finals. Even a Scottish Borderer might have cheered this game, and, when the Blackheath VII., mainly owing to the influence of A. T. Young, led the Harlequins by a goal to nothing at half-time in the other semi-final, the crowd as a whole really began to sit up and take notice. And it was well worth their while to do so, for suddenly there came a real Wakefield try—right through everybody—quickly followed by a typical effort by Hamilton-Wickes at his very best and, finally, a clever try by Worton. Each of these tries was easily converted, and so after all the Harlequins may be said to have justified themselves against fellows of their own size.

Gibbs, for all his outstanding pace, was not so deadly as he might have been if he had joined the three-quarter line more efficiently in their passing movements. Hanging back too far was a fault common to all of the full backs on Saturday, except D. E. Morris, of Blackheath. Morris nearly always was ready to race up on the flanks according to the laws of the Picts and Scots, which alter not—not even to oblige tired Southerners.

Morris scored his side's try against the Harlequins just at the end of the first seven minutes, by backing up one of Young's most brilliant pieces of play. Kendall was Young's chief supporter against Guy's Hospital, who made their effort too late in the game. It was, in fact, noticeable that all of the teams played rather tentatively during the first half and speeded up as they gained in learning and confidence. London Scottish went down to the Harlequins after having a terrific struggle with London Irish that might have ended rather differently had not two of the Irishmen been helped off the field with injured legs. The remaining five Irishmen were not very big men, and they looked even smaller when their number had been reduced to five. One of D. F. Landale's " hands off " nearly accounted for another casualty, and, altogether, one rather felt that the Irishmen's defeat by two goals and a try to nothing was more of an injustice than a beating.

With so many sides involved it was, of course, inevitable that the path towards the final should vary considerably. St. Mary's Hospital, for instance, did splendidly to get so far as they did, but their preliminary tasks were

TEAMS IN FINAL ROUNDS.

BANK OF ENGLAND II.

Forwards :	No.
R. H. Osborne	1
K. A. Macnab	2
H. F. Gilbert	3
Scrum Half :	
J. W. Perts	4
Fly Half :	
E. W. Geipee	5
Threequarter :	
D. G. Mackenzie	6
Full Back :	
R. Fenwick	7
Reserve :	
F. W. Smith	8

Colours: *Blue, white, and old gold.*

BLACKHEATH.

Forwards :	No.
I. M. B. Stuart	7
W. E. Pratten	6
W. E. Tucker	5
Scrum Half :	
A. T. Young	4
Fly Half :	
W. E. W. Kendall	3
Threequarter :	
F. H. X. Gwynne	2
Full Back :	
D. E. Morris	1
Reserve :	
H. R. Saunders	8

Colours: *Black and red hoops.*

GUY'S HOSPITAL.

Forwards :	No.
J. Durr (Capt.)	...
J. Schaboot	...
E. Hutchinson	...
Scrum Half :	
W. Jones	...
Fly Half :	
G. Fellowes Smith	...
Threequarter :	
C. L. Steyn	...
Full Back :	
P. D. B. Spence	...
Reserve :	
G. G. Cameron	...

Colours: *Orange and blue.*

HARLEQUINS.

Forwards :	No.
W. W. Wakefield	7
W. F. Browne	6
J. S. Chick	5
Scrum Half :	
J. R. B. Worton	2
Fly Half :	
V. G. Davies	3
Threequarter :	
R. Hamilton Wickes	4
Full Back :	
J. C. Gibbs	1
Reserve :	
I. J. Pitman	8

Colours: *Light blue, chocolate, french grey and magenta. Sleeves light green and black reversed. White knickerbockers and dark stockings.*

HARLEQUINS II.

Forwards :	No.
C. K. T. Faithfull	5
H. V. Brodie	6
C. G. Stanley	7
Scrum Half :	
F. D. Field-Hyde	3
Fly Half :	
P. Hodge	2
Threequarter :	
H. C. Pattisson	4
Full Back :	
H. C. Laird	1
Reserve :	
Sewell	8

Colours:

KING'S COLL. HOSP.

Forwards :	No.
W. R. F. Collis	...
G. F. Taylor	...
D. A. Collier	...
Scrum Half :	
J. W. Easton	...
Fly Half :	
J. L. Livingstone	...
Threequarter :	
C. J. Farr	...
Full Back :	
W. N. L. Wade	...
Reserve :	
F. Mayo	...

Colours:

Blackheath took part in the first sevens hosted by Middlesex at Twickenham in 1926, and proved a great success. Arthur Young, the England international scrum half, was brilliant at sevens, the game being based on quick thinking and resolute running.

GRAVE IS GAY: AT THE SEVEN-A-SIDE RUGBY MATCHES.

SHORT-TIME, SMALL-TEAM RUGBY: THE HARLEQUINS WIN AGAIN AT TWICKENHAM.

The Seven-a-Side Rugby Tournament organised by the Middlesex County Rugby Union on behalf of the King Edward Hospital Fund was brought to a conclusion before some 10,000 spectators last Saturday at Twickenham. The Harlequins were again successful, running away with the game from Blackheath in the final. In the semi-finals the 'Quins had beaten Richmond and Blackheath the Old Cranleighans.

The game was an instant success in England and when Blackheath returned to Twickenham the following year they improved on their previous performance by reaching the final. Alas, they again fell to defeat against Harlequins.

Club returned to the Twickenham finals in 1930. They had a good season generally, with a number of internationals in the side, and they had even managed to regularly field an 'extra A' fifteen, which contained several first class players.

At Twickenham they again gave good account of themselves. Their second sevens side reached the final, going down 6-0 to London Welsh.

Finally, a strong Blackheath side managed to win the Middlesex Sevens tournament in 1932. Once again their opponents in the final were Harlequins. The Blackheath side pictured here with the referee consists of, from left to right: C. Aarvold, E.J. Hiley (referee), A. Chorlton, J. Tallent, F. Simpson, T. Gubb, B. Black, C. Bailey.

Twickenham had no tannoy announcement system in 1932, save for the gentleman standing at the head of the stairs with a bull-horn! However, everybody in the stadium seemed to be delighted at Blackheath's success.

As big as the Twickenham Sevens are, those played in the Borders of Scotland are still considered to be the major events. When Blackheath went to play at the Galashiels Sevens in the Border Memorial Sevens in 1957 they were the first English side to take part in the thirty-eight year old tournament. They beat Jed Forest in the final to pick up the trophy. Three of the players, Bruce, Douglas and Sharp, were actually Scots.

Blackheath FC
Winners of the Russell Cargill Trophy, Twickenham 1958

Club followed up victory in the Border Sevens by winning the Russell Cargill Trophy again in 1958, with a side skippered by John Williamson. In the final of the event they easily overcame Saracens to win 16-3.

Since those glorious days of the 1950s, Club's sevens successes have been somewhat less outstanding. They did reach the semi-finals of the Hawick Sevens in 1969, but by 1976 had to content themselves with winning the Surrey County Sevens.

Sevens remains an important part of the rugby calendar and, even without having any major recent successes, Blackheath have continued to produce good sevens players, such as Matt Griffiths, pictured here in 1993. In 1996 they shocked mighty Leicester, winning 33-28 at Twickenham in a year that the prize money for the winning side was £50,000. They eventually lost 42-7 to a Barbarians side made up almost exclusively of Fijians.

114

Eight

The Old and the Beautiful

Rugby has always been a social sport. This photograph shows the ubiquitous Charlie Street (with cap) serving up half-time oranges and beer for members of the Veterans, who seem to prefer the traditional method of baulking up. The man with the flag is Peter Piper.

60 years at The Rectory Field

Peter Piper talks to Eddie Pond

It always puzzled me why the football club Sheffield Wednesday is so called. Now I know, for Peter Piper's first game at the Club was for Blackheath Wednesday. In 1936, aged fifteen he turned out as fly half (stand off as they were called in ancient times) for the Wednesday afternoon team whilst still a pupil at the Cherry Orchard Prep. School at Shirley House.

The school was in Cherry Orchard Lane, roughly behind the south east corner of the Rectory Field. He played rugby and cricket for the school, was also a bit of a sprinter and gymnast. Previously he had been a pupil and boarder at St Helen's, the location described as turn left out of Gamberdella's, by the Royal Standard, and you were there. That is probably before Gamberdella's was there though. As they opened in 1927 we are talking about the olden days, when policemen wore top hats and Henry the Eighth was meeting Anne Boleyn in Greenwich Park. Why he had to board when he only lived in Vanbrugh Fields leaves a lot to be explained.

Hearing of Peter's prowess at rugby, he was poached by Oundle, the famous public school near Northampton where he gained further honours as a sportsman and very little as a scholar. He was an Under Officer in the cadet corps which stood him in good stead later when he became a captain in the Home Guard. Most of the plots in Dad's Army must have come from him. At this time he was working in Wallsend, near Newcastle, as a ship building apprentice. He helped build the aircraft carrier Anson, played rugby for Swan Hunter and the College of Commerce, and was twice picked for Northumberland/Durham versus Cumberland/Westmoreland. He would have played for them more often if only he could speak the language they talk up there, which is just like when Mickey Skinner gets excited.

After the war, Peter returned to work in Greenwich for the family firm of lightermen and ship repairers and eventually becoming Master of the Company of Watermen and Lightermen of the River Thames. In this position he ran the Doggett's Coat and Badge rowing race with the Master of the Fishmonger's Company which he describes in his own inimitable manner as "B..... boring".

He lived with and in awe of his grandfather who had built up J.R.Piper Ltd from nothing, with little or no schooling, spelling yacht - yot - in spite of racing his own yachts at Cowes.

When he asked grandfather for time off to get married he was told he could have Saturday morning. He was married in Newcastle on Saturday afternoon, spent one honey moon night at the Bromley Court Hotel and was back at work on his bike on Monday. That must have been when you could go to the cinema, buy a pint and a packet of fags, get fish and chips, and still have some change from a shilling.

Peter's wife Dorothy was well known at the Club, for she made mini suppers for both the rugby and cricket teams. When Peter joined Swan Hunter's as a nineteen year old straight from school during war time he found the drawing office full of women whose husbands and boy friends were off in the forces and realised he had struck gold. In fact, he gave the office boy five shillings to get Dorothy's address which he considers to be the best investment he ever made. Certainly better than his investment in Lloyds.

This all leads up to the historic first post war game, nineteen days after the war ended, when the combined Blackheath and Richmond Clubs played Northampton at the Richmond Athletic Ground on Saturday 22 September, losing 5 - 17. The programme price two pence shows Piper at stand off, G.F.Smith, a past president, in the pack, and Moore, who was to become Lord Phillip Moore, at full back. As Moore played for England at wing forward it suggests a versatility or non specialization, sadly lacking from the present day game.

The Rectory Field was unusable for some time following the war having been used as a barrage balloon site. Piper, or 'Pipes', as he now became known played for the combined side against London Welsh, Wasps, Rosslyn Park and Leicester, as stand off, wing and/or centre. He says he played in the first game back at the Rectory Field but cannot remember when it was. He played in the Club's centenary celebration match against Rugby School and many times with immediate Past President Hugh Neely, who he says was 'a b..... sight more mad than he is now'.

Peter once asked the famous Doctor Neely if he felt proud to have his two sons Hugh and Clive playing together in the Blackheath team, to which he received the reply 'Proud? They're both b..... fools."

Sports men wanting to play past their peak is not a new phenomenon. The Blackheath Veterans side regularly played against the Bank of England in the 1920s and '30s. Before that an 'Old Crocks' side would play annually. These teams nearly always contained players that had recently represented their countries.

Peter Piper first played rugby for Blackheath in 1936, aged fifteen. He had captained every side, excluding the First XV, and went on to found the Golden Oldies, even taking an England team to Bermuda in 1988 for the inaugural Golden Oldies World Cup.

Old at 35? Certainly Not!

COME thirty-five many sports activists have, or are thinking about calling it a day. The body has perhaps taken enough knocks, speeds are slowing down, injury rates are increasing and the mind is not as responsive as it once was.

Talk to anybody from Blackheath's Banshees, however, and you will discover their belief that life begins at 35.

The Banshees (the name is an anagram of Has Beens), are Blackheath's veterans side, which was formed in 1981 for those who refused the option of carpet slippers simply because they couldn't get first team rugby.

In fact the Banshees was set up at a time when organisation at Blackheath's Rectory Field was not quite as slick as it is now. One man was trying to organise six teams, and was basically failing. The Club's sixth outfit in those days had no name and precious little organisation. Very much a social side it did provide a clearing house for new players.

Two of the Banshees regular players, Paul Gay and Baron Phillips decided to take the situation by the scruff of the neck. "It's had its ups and downs, " says Phillips, "and it still relies on the captain and the secretary, but the Club is much better run now. We established a hard core

of about 10 players and the rest was made up as we went along. We weren't vets at the time, just the last team. One guy turned up for a game on spec, played for the Banshees and six weeks later was in the firsts. That's how adhoc the whole thing was."

Although the Banshees started out as the sixth team it has developed into a fully-fledged vets. side. "We decided to grow into a vets team," laughs Phillips. Now it is an established part of the club, and indeed very much a social, and sociable side with players and their wives mixing socially outside of the club.

The development of the Banshees, under Gay's watchful eye, means that the team now tours abroad, gives support to the first team and provides rugby for genuine former first teamers. One of the current Banshees line up, Peter Bullock, was the first team captain when the Banshees was formed. "That is precisely the thing we wanted to create," says Phillips.

For many people who play what are classed as spectator sports, it is still the participation aspect that is important. To suggest retirement at 35 to these people, whatever their standard is not likely to receive a good response. "We tend to view rugby as a players sport rather than one for spectators." Just as well, Baron, the picture on the right is not a pretty one.

Dirty old men, aka The Banshees

A more regular Veterans side in latter years has been the Banshees (an anagram of 'has beens'). The side, formed in 1981, plays regular games, often on a Saturday morning so that they can watch the first team in the afternoon. This picture and story are from 1995.

From the Banshees' inception they had a proud record of eight years without winning on tour. This kick by Bruce Holcombe eventually brought victory against Aberavan's third team, who had not lost all season.

All smiles for the 1993 Banshees, skippered by Peter Brown. Paul Gay (front row, second from the right) helped establish the side. With the emphasis on fun, the team's touring motto, in keeping with their name, was 'Having a wail of a time.'

There is still the serious and energetic work of rugby to consider, however. This side, pictured in around 1996, are clearly not in a fit shape to continue the battle. Albert Patrick (walking right to left in the picture) has also represented Scotland at wrestling in the Commonwealth Games, being given the honour of carrying the national flag at the opening ceremony.

Blackheath's women's team came into existence in 1992 and was skippered by Maxine Edwards. The club had previously been attached to Bromley RFC and already contained a number of international players. Since then it has established itself as an integral part of the Club at the Rectory Field. Training nights are taken very seriously by the women, who also know how to get a social event moving. As with the men's side, the women have, at times, suffered from losing talented players to teams with better resources, but a strong sense of camaraderie has kept the side fairly buoyant. Many of the players attend first team matches on Saturdays, helping out with matchday tasks and generally giving the club fantastic support.

One of the women's most successful players has been Jacquie Edwards, a former pupil at Crofton School. Edwards took part in the 1994 Women's World Cup in Scotland, bathing herself in glory by scoring a spectacular try for England in the final. No less than six Blackheath players took part in the tournament.

In 1995 the women's team was asked to do some modelling for *Marie Claire* magazine, thus proving the adage that there are no glamorous women involved in rugby a lie.

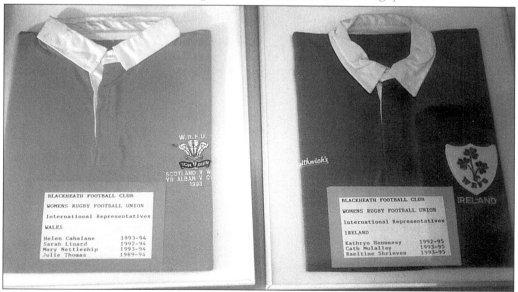

Fun and frivolity is often the hall-mark of the women's section at Blackheath, but behind it all is a successful set of rugby players. International shirts are just as prized for women as they are for men.

The women's section regained their First Division status when they won promotion at the end of the 1998/99 season. They are pictured here collecting the ball in the line-out in the final game, a victory against Saracens' second side at the Rectory Field. Note the large crowd that had turned up in support.

Celebrating success is part of the game at Blackheath. Kathryn Hennessy, an Irish international who helped found the original side that started playing at Bromley, is basking in the glory of the 1998/99 success (back row, fifth from the right).

Nine

The Future's Bright in Red and Black

For any club to progress in the modern world of sport they must look after their young charges. This particular set of young hopefuls are the club's 1998/99 under-9s side, glorious in victory at the London Irish festival. They went through the season playing 37 games without defeat and without a try being scored against them.

On Sunday mornings Greenwich Park is awash with young rugby players in various stages of training with Blackheath. Phil Ubee, Club's first team coach (seen here in the right background of the picture), is watching this young side.

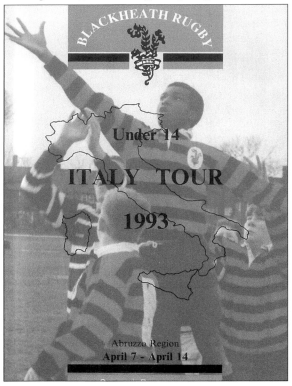

Touring is part of the tradition of young rugby just as much as the senior game. Tours are partially financed by the mini-section producing glossy tour souvenirs which are sold prior to the tour as well as taken away on the tour itself.

The rules of the game are made simpler for those of a younger age, but this under-14s side is well versed in the art of packing down for the scrum.

Getting it right in the line-out is not always easy, even for seniors. The same under-14s side's forwards struggle in 1993.

Oliver Slow and Ben Clewley, seen here playing for the under-9s in 1994/95, have both moved on to the under-13s side. How far will they go?

Joe Bonner is part of the England under-18s set up. No doubt Oliver Slow and Ben Clewlcy would like to emulate him. Tight head prop Bonner will no doubt want to go one better than former Club hero Mick Harris and play in a full international match.

Stefano Ancora (pictured front) skippered the Blackheath under-18s side in 1998/99, gaining two Italian under-19s caps in the process. Like Bonner he has already trained with the first team squad, much being expected of him in the future.

Acknowledgements

It would be quite impossible to assemble a book such as this without much help from many people. My biggest debt of thanks goes to Peter Brown, who did much of the leg work in contacting individuals and getting hold of their photographs. Peter helped me sort out the order of the book and even provided some of the pictures himself. His wife, Mandy Allen, should also be thanked heartily for contacts, suggestions, photographs and scrumptious breakfasts provided while working on the project.

For the provision of photographs and memorabilia I am indebted to: Frank Clodd, Bert Street, David Heald, Mike Williams, Rick Whiteman, Jack Montgomery, Peter Piper, Eddie Pond, Peter Morris, Neil Rhind, Mick Harris, Tom Morris, Matt Stewart, Peter Brown, Mandy Allen, Kelly O'Lyons and Jack Kay.

I trust I have offended no one nor broken any copyright. As a professional journalist, I know what copyright means to people – a living – and I do not wish to take food from anybody's mouth.